ORCHID ELEGY

MATTHEW GASDA

© 2017 by Matthew Gasda
Book design © 2017 by Sagging Meniscus Press

All Rights Reserved.

Printed in the United States of America.
Set in Adobe Garamond with LaTeX.

ISBN: 978-1-944697-23-5 (paperback)
ISBN: 978-1-944697-24-2 (ebook)
Library of Congress Control Number: 2016915806

Sagging Meniscus Press
web: http://www.saggingmeniscus.com/
email: info@saggingmeniscus.com

A precise language awaits a completed metaphysics.
A.N. Whitehead

Basically it's none of our business how somebody manages to grow, if only he does grow, if only we're on the trail of the law of our own growth…
Rainer Maria Rilke

While a new lead is developing, the rhizome may start its growth again from a so-called 'eye,' an undeveloped bud, thereby branching.
Wikipedia

Yet mark'd I where the bolt of Cupid fell:
It fell upon a little western flower,
Before milk-white, now purple with love's wound,
And maidens call it love-in-idleness.
William Shakespeare

We carry within us the wonders we seek without us.
Thomas Browne

Orchid

Elegy

1 Petals like
    characters in a play.

2 Healing the body away:
    like the revisions of the early Schumann
    by the late Schumann.

3 Exposed nerve of the
    crushed flower—cut
    into light.

4 Frozen like a songbird
    caught dead in winter:
    let go of nothing that
    does not heal.

5 'I hold the river of
    you upon my eyelids
    when I cannot sleep.'

6   Now a black sound falling
    from the atmosphere: rain
    on the drum of the earth.

7   It was along the secret
    of your skin: flower-rooted white-
    ankled Eurydice,
    spinning back into smoke.

8   Like a möbius strip or
    whatever you were: jointed between
    words, twisting
    around the poignancy of grief.

9   Your skin thrown over
    a delicate muscle (flower
    of Eleusis, barley seed,
    unformed stem): 'so lift the trees
    & raise the dead.'

10 Like eyes foaming
under cold water: petals,
poor as nature, pressed
against themselves
in the cold.

11 Turn back the bookpetals,
chalkwhite, like the sails
of a Greek ship lost in a
vacuum of stars they
call the Kosmos.

12 Replete in your shell, dishevelled
with life: an earthenware
jar placed at the threshold of silence.

13   Dislocated & bent back
     together: because so
     much is uncertain
     when spring vanishes
     like a dancer
     from the ballroom.

14   Sanatorium glass: internalized
     in the mind—this
     is what you look through
     (a lacerated sadness).

15   Because poems without names
     still long to be touched.

16   A bloom like hands
     drawn away from the face.

17   & so
you broke
the bones of the heart.

18   Flowing north, like
iron in a bowl of water:
aiming to find the world that is.

19   Your pollen
grains held together
by a glue-like alkaloid:
rudely formed, blue as a
cornflower's.

20   Yet it was the rain
that was torn
to pieces by the shape
of the light.

21 Demeter-lure
    (*physis*,
    lost-one),
    sorrowing mother—
    searching for traces of
    frost
    on the grass.

22 Then your muscles tense
    & release like an infant's
    hand around its mother's finger.

23 & if it were not
    for the silhouettes I
    see of you I
    would designate you
    as no one (a lonely
    moon pulling at
    our tides).

24   A noise
      made
      in the slashing open
      of your music.

25   The ghost of a mental
      flower: ankles
      turned, ligaments
      hurt: calyx-mouth
      open like the obscure
      metaphor of pain.

26   Self-sustaining, far
      from the sea, like
      a little radio play:
      & slowly the
      poem emerges from
      its secret.

27 Tipsy nerves
    curving along
    the center
    of your stem:
    quietly fading
    towards the resemblance
    of a name.

28 Fireflies
    sweeping
    across
    the river
    outside &
    there is no
    biological
    grammar
    which accounts
    for the cinema
    inside of thinking.

29 The petals of her eyes
    floating up like drowned
    ships suspended inside
    of poetic loss: 'because
    the wound is the place
    where the light enters you.'

30 Like a bird at sea
    answering through
    a circle in the ear,
    or a dress, open
    at the waist.

31 Having fulfilled in
    you nothing which I
    was looking for (& everything
    which I was).

32 I placed my hands on
    your ribs,
    breathed through your
    lungs: tasted the flesh of poetry
    between your teeth, touched
    the bright Narcissi
    in your hair.

33 A figure or face, shedding gravity
    like water—we
    dare not cross the almost
    Orphic protection
    which surrounds you.

34 Like petals which
    touch lovingly
    as they remember themselves.

35 Where the moon strikes
    the throat's tissue: evoked
    in the bare, radiant
    manifestation of a signature
    beyond all context.

36 Out of the slender
    emptiness
    like a swaying lover, girted
    round by night.

37 The brain is
    silent: a snow of
    neurons falls over
    a map of everything
    we've lost.

38   You were dislocated
     from the earth during a
     flowerless spring &
     we were unused to
     hearing such emotion
     in your voice.

39   So everything is carried away: ritual-tree,
     Bodi-tree—& we
     are bound in a strange
     night: never closer,
     never free.

40   Poems made of orchid-
     petals (& the most
     important category
     of beauty is the beauty
     of that which is lost).

41 Memory's translucent sheath around the blackened flower of the heart.

42 Petal-like around the single pistil: an aporia of the present.

43 Self-enclosed on open terrain: listening to the acoustics of disavowed need.

44 You wade
towards the spring perpetually spiraling &
almost dead, beautiful Orpheus
laying there on the banks
of the river.

45 Water is your meta-
figure: folded
along the convex
of your shell.

46 I gave you teeth:
fitted them
to your hands—
to the fragments of the earth
we are made of.

47   Accomplishing a
     repression of every
     instinct of grief (because
     words have no other
     meaning for us).

48   'I'll collect stars
     in a wooden bowl: scatter
     your petals overtop the
     light, watch them
     clot like proteins in
     soured milk.'

49   Opening like a
     moonrise in reverse:
     your eyes close
     against me.

50 Foundling
    language—
    silo for capturing
    the future—
    pearl-pale,
    leaves not
    wider than a
    knife-back.

51 'So an Odysseus is
    always charting the stars
    finding his way back home—despite
    himself.'

52 A semantics joined
    at the navel of speech, a braid
    of grammars inside the poem
    (& things which matter most
    should never be at the mercy of
    the things which matter least).

53 Chora: poem of a place,
desert of a desert—emptied of itself.

54 Despite nothing, I'll
scrape a fable from your skin.

55 Like unburying a
body, you would float
towards the world like
a lost balloon.

56 As fragile as body in a
dissection room, or an Orpheus
spinning on his
heels: a devotion which
does nothing but forgive.

57 Growing at a right angle
to the axis of the root & the
analogy extends: deconstructs
the surface of your skin.

58 A sort of cinematic music
    from which the action
    unfurls along
    the spire of the cathedral (which
    plays the role
    of a radio antenna): 'because
    you love the formless:
    the radiant zigzag
    becoming.'

59 A glass Orchid
    pressed between the
    paper of a book: I could not
    love in the company
    of another.

60 So much like
    the lie the curtain

makes when it closes
on the play (& the flowers
of some species supposedly
resemble moths in flight).

61 &
when you shut your lens,
you
begin to see a role
for blindness
in the scaffolding of sight.

62 & so often our dreams
have no explosion or catharsis: no
beginning or end (it's kairos: an opening
    weaving braiding
flower of thought
(& metanoia: the sewing of regret)).

63 A theology of embodied
time (the act of
seeding as grieving)—the undelivered
wound of memory.

64 These dreams in a rainstorm, blind
even unto
unknowingness (askesis:
the logical space of the flower).

65 Objects without verbs
like marble stars
strewn across the floor.

66 Mercy
remembered
in the sunlight
of the mirror.

67 Fractures
   earmarked like re-
   read letters: a tenseless voice
   voiced
   for falling time.

68 The tide rose
   over the cathedral,
   flowering in the mud.

69 Emergent, radiant,
   like mass to matter, concealed
   in the search for
   names: you failed again &
   again to ask
   for what you wanted.

70 Decomposed
fires were swept
from this long
sleep without scars.

71 Phonic lesion, a dislocation
inside the ear—melodies repeat,
cross-referenced in time.

72 Unthreaded spindles laid
on the kitchen table, the
stars spilling out like
grain from a sack.

73 I measured the stripe
around your thighs, washed
you clean like a voyeur
with photographs & letters—

brought you to this permanent
domain of dreamloss
(singing like at a burial).

74 To convey the elasticity
of anguish in cinema: muting
all the images that
do not touch or breath.

75 A soul which surrenders
like a circus animal
under the lights.

76 Thresholds
cluster
at the threshold of
sight.

77 It is incised in the
cortex at the moment
of birth: the data of self-
bewilderment (like a blind
drawn
down across
the street).

78 It stunts between the voids of the
body, drives itself
under the surface of the
beloved: open to the needing
self (closed to what
is feeling).

79 A silence is held back
& released in a
swarm (& I am
for this all-engulfing
hunger).

80 What appears
in the form of tropes
shifts: dilates:
bends
around the general
grammar
of the heart.

81 & you are asleep
in a very real sense: shorn
of persons, gripping
tight to a mountain
of abstraction.

82 You grow where death
perforates
the scaffolding of beauty.

83 'You laid them in
    the sound of place
    & they heard you.'

84 Coronal blood, a
    sun slipped
    under the door.

85 When the cranes
    are folded back into paper, flesh
    & feather are left on the floor.

86 A sacrifice in Sanskrit charged
    with the conjugated verbs of a lost infinity (a
    wheel without spokes: a memory
    turning in the place
    where the poem never was).

87 I baited the stars
    on fishing-line & cast
    them back into
    the water:

88 A thematized
    closeness, like
    the fractal
    of a season
    (spring without
    spring, dreams
    without days).

89 You were a figure danced
    into porcelain &
    you heard without
    listening where
    the memory was
    in the picture-heart.

90 Eleusine grain
    fallen into fire, gathered
    back as loss.

91 This is the slender organism
    from which radiates all the other
    planes of the body: a skeleton
    grafted inside the skin.

92 '& you imagine that it's
    an easy thing, but it's not
    an easy thing—to make
    a world up.'

93 The stars laid out
    like bodies in the grass: so
    offer me language like sleep (give
    rain or take it).

94 Everything is
    folded into the

text, because the soul is
always beautiful when
unreceived.

95 An inwoven pressure
tinged with radiance, suppurated
from the bone
of self-possession: &
what is the color
of what is essentially shimmering?

96 'Because we
feel ashamed
when the dead
return.'

97 Petals, like
soldiers crossing
& uncrossing
the Marne.

98 I traced love
across the surface of
singing—& I saw you,
hearing me.

99 & you were
undestroyed,
like water.

100 Birds split open
at the throat: the
silver bulbs of the
music stolen.

101 Intention drawn
from the shell
of hollow pearl you
called *agape*—
the scarred, tissue
of the brain & mouth.

102 I'll dismember the
other flowers, knead them
back into your flesh (so
that you can be lovely
again).

103 Cut carefully around
the flower: be careful not
to ruin the thin, almost
liquid membrane of its skin.

104 Bubbling
through the light's surface:
the fractal of
the light.

105 The eye of the Orchid
opens: becomes
the space of memory.

106 & culled from
absence,
you still
throw me
at every turn.

107 Skin black with oil &
milk when I
catch you & pin your
wings to the floor.

108 Overlapping petals
folded
like honeycombs:
because
self-creation is like this
(a burial rite).

109 'but then again I
think I just

wanted to become
adept at being
haunted again.'

110 & the shame is
underneath: it is the
context which you disclaim
as kin.

111 I stood for something
like years, waiting
for the unreleased
parachutes to open.

112 A zero was
circled &
scored—Orphic,
isolated,
understood.

113 In a house without
lights, I'll pluck the music from
your marrow, run
the melodies together, pull
the soul from its sheath.

114 Pulled in two directions at
once like a foregone
conclusion: because consciousness,
as if by magic, has
a contrapuntal texture.

115 Petals flawed
with sunlight, fingers
smeared with mud: the gruel
of winter seed
in our bellies.

116 The moon wears
the skin of the sun turned

inside-out (a blue-bottle mouth
so different than dark,
wild roses).

117 I rinsed you clean in the
heavy water (opened
your mouth with hunger).

118 The bones of the missaid poem
were disinterred &
burned for the sake of closure.

119 Melting like salt in a barrel (the
stars)—& no trace
of love: just the
so-called disorder of beauty.

120 Representing lapses from
the ontological order to
the gentleness the unrevealed: this planet,
sleeping through its orbit.

121 The
smallest
thread
is something
silver
still.

122 Like
a single
ship leaving
the fleet,
desolation
must
be something
like
this:

123 Echoes of
light in parallel
with mourning: as if using
the camera to make paintings
in motion.

124 Naked, grasping the margin of the room—
a summer dress at the
ankles: 'because it's so immensely
difficult to be destroyed
every day by this thing that you are
responsible for loving
anyway—because how could
Love love itself?'

125 Your fingers sliding
around, grasping the sunlit
material of shadow (so just be
careful not to evoke the axioms
of beauty as sin).

126 With the same pathos
that the Greeks employed in
self-revelation: 'because
you expect people to see
everything about
you & they never do.'

127 & yet tropes
survive like viruses:
evolve without
essential structure—

128 Lost love: you have
no name, no copy, no
sound—oozing
through the winter grass.

129 Break
your interiority
like morning bread—

130 Like a Phaedra
burning, daylight tapering
into loss (&
was this nourished only as
love?—this motion which
enjoins you with sight (this
motion which sees you)).

131 A color disassembled—cut
into black ribbons: an improvised
shyness: a backbone
glued
to the future of touch.

132 Drawn
naked—each repetition signals the
body's confinement: like a jug
of milk, waiting to fall
from the table.

133 Look inside the architecture of
a star: it is sung
backwards, as if in a dream.

134 Waves of
disinterested sound (unburied from another
life).

135 Spring
lightsome, wave through
wave—hair down: lost
in the sonority of the earth.

136 The caesura marks
the late hour
of forgiveness.

137 Poignantly I laid your
body out
in the slim dark—& poignantly,
each day began.

138 Shapes arranged
into the fragility of truth: half-
spectral, half-errant.

139 Nude
turned around
in the stairwell—
nothing
is happening
that is not true.

140 Marked
where the soul
leaves through the skin—
untended
wound—
stripped
of its meaning.

141 & you feel so
quiet when
this porous light
rises from
the water.

142 Sparks of gravity
getting you
off the ground.

143 Bruises touched
into rivers &
oceans & no wayfarer marks
the black sun, sunken
into the evening's ooze.

144 In the
middle of a portrait-sitting:
the faded
yellow of the garden more

precarious than your skin: bitterly
deprived of kindness or
care.

145 Probe through
the brain with a poem,
watch it secrete
a cinema of
sleep.

146 It is nothing we admired:
bleached pearl-petals—
atonements on the order of miracles (& you
slept between my thighs,
night after night).

147 Leaves like wild birds—
taking flight.

148 Founded—
or as foundationless as
the rain?—at a deeper level,
language cools inside
of one perfect mould.

149 The April stars—
floating like anemones in
copper pots (& your
letters falling
out of love).

150 Canticle voices—
endlessly
deferred—thematized
as a sexual wound
in the structure
of music.

151 Like a sheet of glass,
about to be
punched through—sepal,
filament, stigma:
imaged.

152 & teeth clenched, a
chimera is born—almost like a
second thought.

153 Lament &
encomium: in a
deeply stratified poem—
consciousness emerges.

154 A gorgeous
disarticulation passes through
the sentence: Orchid, &
time will pare you down.

155 'Because it's a
lie that there's another mind out
there that can run
alongside yours without
losing its breath.'

156 '& why are you
threading yourself through
everyone like a spiritual
needle—except
out of loneliness?'

157 Attis-blood, the wreaths
of violets, potsherds
altering the salience of
your skin (& so
much is lost
in the witness of devotion).

158 Assured, in
your probation, that
the soul
is a structure of forgetting.

159 You were playing
draughts with
the moon when I found you &
asked you to follow me
wherever I was going.

160 Covered you in linen, indicated
the spot where the
waters would return: sang
the whole earth
into an effigy of ordinary love.

161 Almond-eyes, brutal
in the act of leaving.

162 Sweet, the
    grieving rain
    punished into life.

163 A lyric startles suddenly,
    like a bird,
    from the palm of your hand.

164 Clues
    scattered across
    the matrices
    of voice.

165 Why was I not,
    in any light,
    going back?—touring
    the landscape of
    ferocious loss?

166 Propositions dense
    with metaphor: scripts &

       lexicons turned away
       from what you learned
       by heart.

167   Written like in
       a previous book: buried
       in the images of the
       far interior (an elegy
       for the elegy that is yet
       unwritten).

168   Because
       what is
       inexpressible you
       forgive: the immense
       distance of
       a little time.

169 An external object
hidden inside the Orchid?—
like an aria inside
the ear (a soul maybe: beginning
to grow).

170 Dead still inside the
cylinder of the brain: admiring
the privacy of emotions.

171 Asking only for
the return of the ships which disembarked
in the morning of mourning.

172 No—but
a process continues
beyond the margin of the
first person singular—&
you were looking back from

the eye's shyness (& I
saw you).

173 Alert to the grace of
emergence & the sorrow
that enables the thought
to think itself.

174 So the eye
digests the
aesthetics
burrowed inside
of language.

175 The presence of
disquiet is
an estimate of pain: networked—
spread across
you like
lovers on the floor.

176 Blind at the frontier
of an unaccounted-for
fate: only you
may describe this arrival.

177 Translating Time into
the presence
of singular objects (&
the flowers may last two to
three months after which the Orchid
will need to conserve energy for
further leaf bud &
root development).

178 A shared node,
an elliptical
memory: transparent—
shining.

179 So let this book
    be a recitation: a remembering
    of the love that has always run parallel to
        me—
    as a part of me & as
    a part of some other
    as-of-yet unfulfilled debt
    of grief—so
    let this elegy begin.

Matthew Gasda has published two novels, *Moon on Water* and *Sonata for Piano and Violin,* and is an active playwright and director in New York City.